Celebrate the festive season with a splash of color from the scary Monsters images

In this book, you will find lots of images that you can easily remove and send as a greeting cards.

Have fun Coloring and creating your own Halloween story!...

BOO!

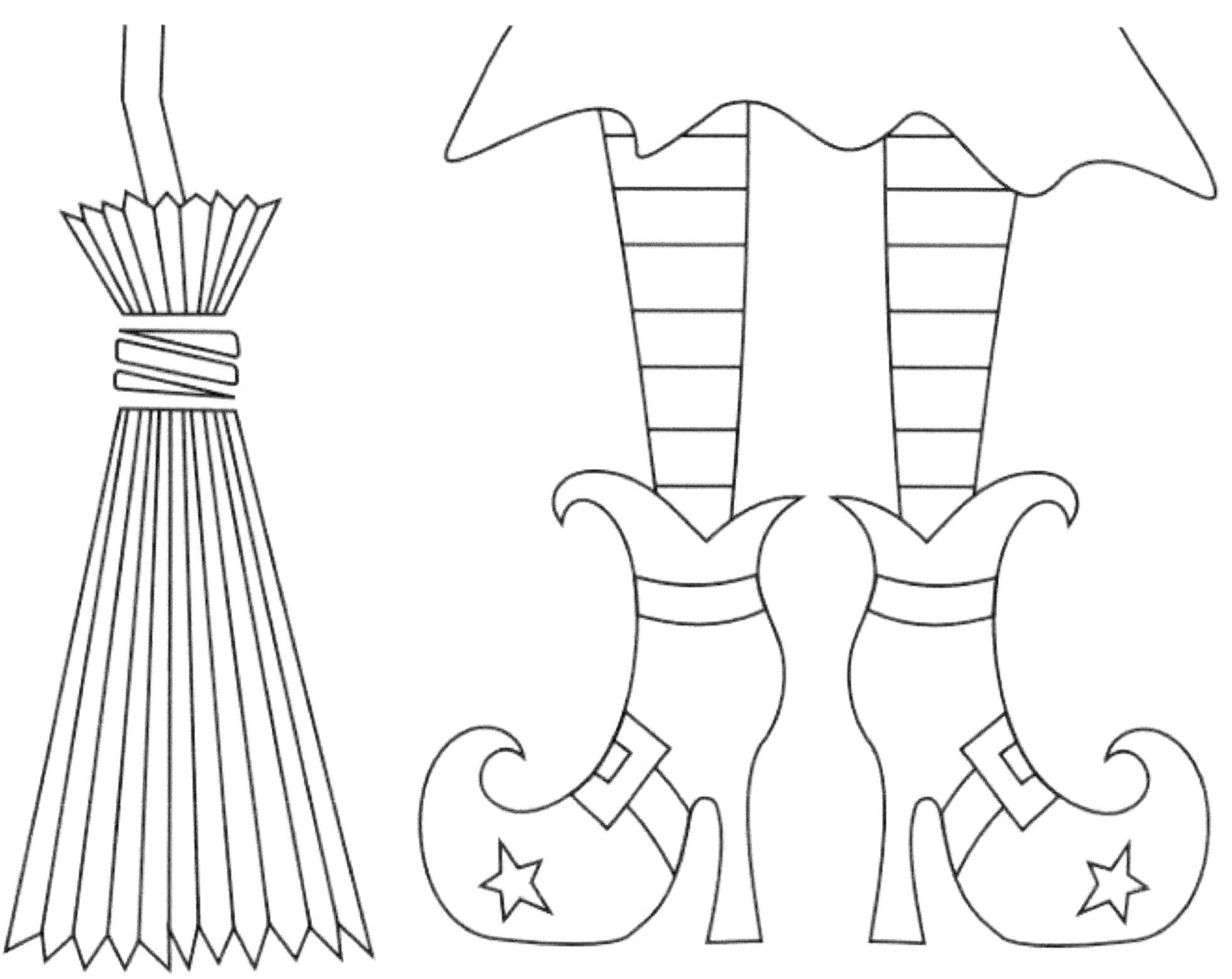

http://coloringoo.com

THE PUMPKIN KING

HAPPY
HALLOWEEN

HALLOWeen

HAPPY
HALLOWEEN

R.I.P.
Halloween Haunted House * Stephany Elsworth * Colorwithsteph.com

HALLOWEEN

BOO!

So Crafty it Hurts

www.ingramcontent.com/pod-product-compliance
Lightning Source LLC
LaVergne TN
LVHW080040170826
845677LV00025B/1864

* 9 7 9 8 8 4 9 9 7 3 9 5 1 *